CORPORATE PROFITS IN COMPANY FINANCIAL REPORTS, TAX RETURNS, AND THE NATIONAL INCOME AND PRODUCT ACCOUNTS

A Study
Produced for the
Financial Executives Research Foundation

by

Norman B. Ture, Inc.

Corporate Profits In
Company Financial Reports, Tax Returns
And The National Income
And Product Accounts

Financial Executives Research Foundation
633 Third Avenue, New York, N.Y. 10017

Library of Congress Catalog Card Number 77-095350
Printed in the United States of America
M 707

First Printing

As the research arm of Financial Executives Institute, the basic objective of the Research Foundation is to sponsor fundamental research and publish authoritative material in the field of business management with particular emphasis on the principles and practices of financial management and its evolving role in the management of business.

Publication of a research study should not be interpreted as constituting endorsement by the Board as a whole, or by individual Trustees.

PROJECT ADVISORY COMMITTEE

Robert L. Cooper, Chairman
INA Corporation

William M. Horne, Jr.
Senior Vice President
Citicorp

Robert E. Lewis
Vice President
Citibank

C. A. Northrop
Controller
International Business Machines Corporation

Richard C. O'Sullivan
Vice President & Treasurer
Monsanto Company

E. A. Vaughn
Executive Vice President
Aluminum Company of America

Benjamin R. Makela
Research Director
Financial Executives Research Foundation

PREFACE

This nation's economic vitality is measured by different yardsticks, and the results — as compiled by government officials, financial writers, and economists — are often contradictory and confusing. One generally accepted component of the country's economic health is the aggregate of corporate profits for any one year. Yet, there are different concepts as to how these corporate profits should be measured.

The three most common measurements of corporate profits are (1) the net income reported by corporations in annual reports and other public documents, (2) the taxable net income reported by corporations to the Internal Revenue Service, and (3) the data computed by the Bureau of Economic Analysis of the Department of Commerce, which is responsible for the development of the National Income and Product Accounts which serve as a key input for many government decisions on fiscal matters.

Corporate executives understand the need for differences between reported net income and taxable net income. But very few people, in or out of government, know how to reconcile either of these amounts reported by corporations with those calculated by the BEA for the National Income and Product Accounts. The differences between the three sets of data are often substantial, and this fact by itself creates confusion in the minds of some of those to whom these data are imporant. Further, the NIPA data are revised annually for a period of years, and this also causes misgiving on the part of those who read the BEA reports by incorrectly assuming that corporations are "monkeying with the figures." This cannot be the case. The changes arise only as a result of revised estimates by the BEA.

This research study was commissioned by the Trustees of the Research Foundation in the expectation that an objective review of the conceptual differences in the various methods of calculating corporate profits would contribute to a better understanding of how this all-important measure of economic vitality is developed. The Trustees also hoped that the researcher, in his investigations, would develop suggesstions for improvements in the method by which corporate net income is determined for NIPA purposes.

This study should be useful in providing an understanding of the differences in methods of calculating corporate profits. It is hoped that the researcher's recommendations for improving the NIPA estimates of corporate net income will be carefully considered.

The Foundation expresses its appreciation to Dr. Norman B. Ture for his careful and objective research, to officials of the Bureau of Economic Analysis who reviewed and offered critical and helpful comments on this study, and to the members of the Project Advisory Committee

K. S. Axelson
President, FERF

TABLE OF CONTENTS

TABLES

FIGURE

CORPORATE PROFITS IN COMPANY FINANCIAL REPORTS, TAX RETURNS, AND THE NATIONAL INCOME AND PRODUCT ACCOUNTS

Introduction: The Occasion and Focus of this Study

The term "corporate profits" has various meanings, measures, and uses, the distinctions among which, unfortunately, are not generally known. The frequent revisions in the Federal Government's National Income and Product Accounts (NIPA) estimates of corporate profits, the most widely disseminated measure, are a source of confusion and sometimes doubts about the accuracy and reliability of corporate profits as reported to company shareholders and to the investment community.

A central issue with which this study is concerned is whether the variance in the NIPA estimates of corporate profits is attributable to the unreliability of business accounting practices and financial reports or whether it is the result of the way in which the estimates are prepared for the NIPA. The study seeks to show how and why the National Income and Product Accounts estimates of corporate profits differ from other concepts and measures of this type of income and to examine and explain the reasons for the frequent and often substantial changes in these estimates.

The results of our study show that the variability in NIPA estimates of corporate profits has no necessary relevance in evaluating the reliability of the alternative measures. We find that however good, bad, or indifferent business accounting practice may be, hence whatever the accuracy and reliability of corporate reports to shareholders, it is not reflected by nor is it the reason for the changes in NIPA estimates of profits. Fundamentally, the variability of the NIPA estimates of profits derives from the estimating procedures themselves. Early estimates of NIPA profits for a given year are based on extrapolations of an earlier year's profits for tax purposes; the extrapolations rely on estimates of rates of change in book profits (i.e., profits reported in corporation financial statements) or in various proxies therefor. Tax, book, and NIPA profits, however, differ materially in concept and measure. The early estimates, in other words, entail the use of three quite different concepts and measures of profits, relying on the assumption that all three consistently change in the same proportion. As a later part of this discussion shows,[1] this is a shaky assumption, indeed.

On the basis of our study, we do *not* conclude that the NIPA estimates are so poor as to be of little use for the basic purpose for which they are made, viz., to show the distribution of the National Income among its several claimants. We do conclude, however, that all interested groups in the society should appreciate the fact that their evaluations of the reliability of the NIPA profits estimates have no necessary implications for the reliability of corporate profits as reported to shareholders.

The reliability of the NIPA estimates is not merely or even chiefly an academic concern. Quantitative information is an essential input into the decision-making that guides all economic activity. To be sure, the care with which data are assembled, evaluated, and used in decision-making varies greatly; so, too, does the quality and quantity of the

[1]See below, pp. 28-39.

information used. And although the quality of information and the skill with which it is used do not uniquely determine economic outcomes, it is surely the case that better data enhance effective decision-making while poor data impair efficiency.

Decision-making, of course, concerns the future, whether near-term or longer range. Information inputs into decision-making pertain to the past; we can make estimates about the future, but facts, in their very essence, are history. We use historical data as the basis for expectations about the future; the past informs us about the context of phenomena, about fundamental relationships, about trends and deviations therefrom, all of which are used in arriving at judgments about the possible outcomes of a course of action.

It is from this perspective that economic data must be evaluated. As a record of the past, recent or remote, these data do not tell us the immediate or more distant future, but they provide us with the building blocks for expectations, for discriminating among possible outcomes, hence for guiding decision-making. The usefulness of the record of the past in formulating anticipations about the future depends, obviously, on the stability of basic economic relationships — on the confident assumption that economic results are not haphazard and that, barring outside shocks, the trends and relationships described by the historical record may be projected into the future. If the data pertaining to specified periods are poor, however, the utility of the record of the past for this purpose is diminished, no matter how stable the economic relationships which determined the actual past outcomes and which will determine those of the future. In other words, if data do not accurately describe past outcomes and the activity which produced them, they are of limited use as a means for formulating expectations about the future.

Quantitative economic information not only enters into the determination of expectations about the future, however; it is also the essential input into evaluations of how well or poorly the economy and its various sectors and subsectors have operated, hence into judgments about future courses of action to improve performance. The record of the performance of the economy as a whole — for example, how much total output it produced, how fully and efficiently the available production inputs were used, etc. — should assist public policy-makers in evaluating the impact of government activity on the economy and the adequacy of public policies for achieving their goals. The same thing is true for the household. To be sure, a significant amount of household economic activity is impulsive rather than carefully considered, and many of its economic outcomes are in part the results of luck, fortuitous developments, and offsetting mistakes. Notwithstanding, households formulate plans and do so upon the basis of expectations which are largely extensions of the past. The more and better information people have about past outcomes, the greater their capacity to evaluate their past performance and to plan to improve it.

By the same token, corporate managers want to know about operating results in order to determine whether the results met their expectations, to identify difficulties and mistakes, and to make plans for better performance in the coming operating periods. Corporate shareholders want to know these results in order to evaluate managerial performance, to assist them in their role as the corporation's electorate, to guide them in their investment decisions, and to improve the results of their investments. Decision-makers in financial institutions need to know these results to assess the soundness of their lending and investment policies and as inputs into their determinations of appropriate portfolio policies. Government officials rely on these results in the evaluation of a wide range of public policies and as the basis for projections about the future magnitude of profits in formulating new policies or in revising existing ones.

Economic data are not self-generating but are the outcome of information-producing activity. They may well or poorly describe the phenomena to which they pertain. Regrettably, there are too often few criteria which data users can rely upon to assess the quality of information. The ultimate tool, one's own perception of the phenomenon, is generally not feasible. No one can perceive the flow of an economy's total output in a year's time; one cannot oneself know, from having taken one's own count of output, what the gross national product was in some given year. One must rely on the data output of those whose business it is to measure economic phenomena. One can partially evaluate the quality of data in terms of a) their stability; is the measure of the phenomenon of some past period frequently and/or materially revised? b) their consistency regarding their conceptual or substantive content; is the definition of the measured phenomen frequently or materially revised? c) the generality of their conceptual or substantive content; is the definition of the phenomenon one which is generally or widely known and agreed upon? and d) the adequacy of the procedures and techniques used for gathering the data; since few pieces of data are derived from censuses, are the sampling procedures and the statistical techniques used to provide the data so designed as to produce acceptable levels of accuracy? Evaluations of this sort, it is obvious, far exceed the capabilities of most of us who receive and use economic data; more precisely, the costs we would have to incur to obtain such evaluations far exceed the benefits to be derived from using such evaluations to help in discriminating among the data. We tend, instead, to rely on the reports of those producing the data and to accept the data as reported.

In the light of these evaluation standards, the economic data produced by Federal Government agencies, for the most part, come off well. There are, to be sure, changes in definition and in sampling procedures from time to time, but in the usual case these changes are infrequent and are aimed at making the data more reliable and useful to a larger number of users. Most data series are from time to time revised, but for the most part such revisions are comparatively small in relative magnitude.

A notable exception is afforded by government estimates of corporate profits. Various government agencies compile estimates of the profits of corporations in the industries over which they have regulatory or oversight responsibilities. By far the most widely disseminated corporate profits estimates and those with the most influence among public and private users, however, are those made by the Bureau of Economic Analysis in the U.S. Department of Commerce. These estimates are components of the National Income and Product Accounts (NIPA) estimates; they are compiled and published both for the total corporate business population and for specific industries. In terms of the criteria sketched above, these data series fare poorly, indeed: the estimates for any given time period are frequently and often substantially revised;

the conceptual content changes, though with far less frequency than the estimates themselves; the NIPA concept differs significantly and in quantitatively substantial extent from that which is generally perceived in the business community to represent profits and these differences are not widely known; and finally, the estimating procedures themselves account for a significant part of the variability in the estimates.

How well or poorly the NIPA estimate corporate profits, either in the aggregate or for one or more industries, has little direct or immediate impact on most people; indeed, relatively few of us have any knowledge of these estimates. The indirect consequences, however, are significant for a great many people. For one thing, estimates of corporate profits are among the key inputs in a wide range of public policy decisions, the implementation of which in government programs and activities is likely to affect the composition and possibly the aggregate level of economic activity, hence to affect most, if not all, businesses and households. Budgetary policy, for example, relies on projections of national income components, including corporate profits, to estimate tax revenues under existing tax laws and to determine whether changes in the government's revenues or expenditures are called for. These revenue projections are made by reference to extrapolations and adjustments of estimates of the national income components in the recent past. Inaccurate estimates of profits in the recent past tend to result in erroneous projections of profits into the near future; they are misleading inputs into policy-making and, accordingly, may adversely affect the economic circumstances of all of us.

These estimates also influence saving and investment behavior in the private sector. As suggested, the estimates for the preceding year importantly influence expectations about profits in the current and succeeding periods. The NIPA estimates, of course, do not provide information about the profits of specific companies, the focus of individuals' investment decisions. But by suggesting the direction of change and magnitude of aggregate profits or those of specific industries, these estimates color the investment outlook, the broad context in which specific investment decisions are made.

In this respect, doubts about the reliability of the estimates diminish their usefulness in building expectations about the future course of profits. Frequent and significant changes in the estimates of past periods' profits raise such doubts.

Perhaps the greatest hazard created by the changes in NIPA estimates of corporate profits for past periods is that they tend to arouse suspicions about the accuracy and reliability of corporations' reports to their shareholders. Any loss in confidence about profits as reported by corporations, resulting from the frequency and magnitude of the changes in NIPA estimates of profits, is likely to have a deleterious effect on the investment climate and to impair the efficiency with which private saving is allocated to the myriad capital formation uses.

The very frequency and magnitude of the changes in the NIPA estimates, however, urge that they are not attributable to deficiences in business accounting practices. Whatever those deficiencies, if any, might be, it is difficult to perceive how they could have resulted in four different NIPA estimates, issued in the first seven months of 1976, of 1975 corporate profits before taxes or how they might have accounted for the fact that the January estimate of $119.8 billion exceeded the July estimate by $5.3 billion.[2] In fact, these NIPA revisions are attributable to the procedures used to estimate profits for NIPA purposes.

It is, of course, possible that the differences in the concepts of profits for NIPA, for tax purposes, and for business accounting and the changes in each over time might explain some of the variance in the NIPA estimates of profits for a given year. On the whole, however, these changing conceptual differences appear to account for few of the estimate-to-estimate changes in the NIPA. Even were this not the case, however, the magnitude of the change in the NIPA estimates would have no necessary bearing on the quality of business accounting practice, unless it were deemed to be good only if it were immutable. Without a general appreciation of the sources of variance in the NIPA estimates and of

---

[2]Cf. U.S. Department of Commerce, Bureau of Economic Analysis, *Survey of Current Business,* issues for the months of January through July, 1976.

the limited use made in the preparation of those estimates of the financial reports prepared by corporate management for stockholders, however, the frequent and substantial changes in the NIPA estimates may give rise to suspicions about business accounting practices.

The purposes of this study do not include a searching examination and evaluation of business accounting practices. The principal concerns, rather, are to delineate the concept of profits which NIPA attempt to measure, to explain how this concept differs from others used in measuring the results of corporate operations, to note and to quantify in detail the change in NIPA estimates of profits, and to explain the reasons for the frequency and magnitude of the changes in these estimates.

Alternative Concepts of Profits

As stated above, the term "profits" has various meanings. The differences in these meanings do not reflect misapprehensions or conceptual deficiencies, although each definition presents its own difficulties. Rather they reflect primarily the difference in purposes for which the measurement of profits is undertaken. By the same token, differences in measured profits do not indicate that one measure is "correct" and the others are "wrong"; the correctness of each can be ascertained only against the concepts upon which it is based. The fact that book profits of a company — the profits it reports to its shareholders and to the Securities and Exchange Commission and/or other government agencies — differ from its profits for tax purposes does not imply that one is "true" and the other is in error.[3]

These differences in concept and measurement are so numerous and varied as to preclude their detailed listing and explanation in this study. Instead, a number of the major differences are examined to illustrate the contentions stated just above.

---

[3]Conceptual and measurement differences are also found in other income claims. For example, labor compensation as measured in the NIPA differs from that as measured for tax purposes, as calculated by business employers, as perceived by its recipients, and as conceived in economic theory.

Corporate Profits in the National Income and Product Accounts

The measurement of profits in the NIPA derives from the central objective of these accounts, viz., to measure the value and composition of the output of goods and services in the economy (and its various sectors and subdivisions) and the various income claims or charges thereupon.[4] Since the aggregate of all income claims must just equal the value of aggregate production measured in the NIPA, and since the value of aggregate production is necessarily equal to the aggregate costs of production, each class of income in the NIPA defines payments for production inputs. Profits in the NIPA are the payments for the input of the services of the capital which is owned by corporation shareholders. As one of the income claims on the value of the period's output, NIPA profits are a measure of the value of the production services provided by corporate equity capital.

Implementing this concept in quantitative terms results in a number of important differences from the measurement of profits on a corporation's books. Since NIPA profits relate only to the period's flow of services and the output attributable thereto, they do not include valua-

	1976 billions of $
A. All Corporations	
1. All corporations — corporate profits with inventory valuation and capital consumption adjustments	117.8
2. All corporations — corporate profits with inventory valuation adjustment and without capital consumption adjustment	133.3
3. All corporations — profits before tax	147.9
4. All corporations — profits after tax	83.6
5. All corporations — corporate profits with inventory valuation and capital consumption adjustments: profits after tax	53.5
6. All corporations — corporate profits before deduction of capital consumption allowances with inventory valuation adjustment	230.6

---

[4]Actually, the NIPA customarily present a number of alternative measures of corporate profits, representing differing concepts and coverage. The April 1977 issue of the *Survey of Current Business*, for example, includes in various tables the following measures of profits for 1976:

B. **Domestic Corporations**

7. Domestic corporations — corporate profits with inventory valuation and capital consumption adjustments	110.3
8. Domestic industries — corporate profits with inventory valuation adjustment and without capital consumption adjustment	125.8
9. Domestic corporations — profits before tax	140.4
10. Domestic corporations — profits after tax	76.0
11. Domestic industries — corporate profits before deduction of capital consumption allowances with inventory valuation adjustment	223.1

C. **Nonfinancial Corporations**

12. Nonfinancial corporations — corporate profits with inventory valuation and capital consumption adjustments	95.8
13. Nonfinancial corporations — corporate profits with inventory valuation adjustment and without capital consumption adjustment	111.4
14. Nonfinancial corporations — profits before tax	126.0
15. Nonfinancial corporations — profits after tax	72.0
16. Nonfinancial corporations — corporate profits before deduction of capital consumption allowances with inventory adjustment	203.6

As the groupings in the table indicate, separate measures of profits are shown for all U.S. corporations, all domestic corporations, and for nonfinancial domestic corporations. Included in the first set of profit measures are the repatriated earnings, net of foreign taxes, of foreign subsidiaries and the after-tax profits of foreign branches of U.S. corporations. The second grouping shows profits of U.S. corporations derived solely from operations within the United States; it excludes profits of foreign-owned companies in the United States. The third grouping shows profits from the domestic operation of U.S. corporations in industries other than those classified as "financial."

Within each grouping, several measures of profits are shown. While most nearly coinciding with the business accounting concepts, the measures labeled "profits before tax" and "profits after tax" differ in important respects from the corresponding business accounting measures. Profits before tax is, in effect, the base from which the other measures shown are derived.

tion changes. Thus, they are adjusted to eliminate the effects of changes in the valuation of inventories.[5] The inventory valuation adjustment (IVA) attempts to measure the difference between the change in the physical volume of nonfarm business inventories, measured in prices

[5]The NIPA also present an alternative measure — profits before tax — which is not adjusted for changes in the value of inventories.

of the current period, and the change in the book value of nonfarm inventories. This adjustment is necessary to conform the measurement of this component of total output to that of the others. Since the sum of the income claims on total output must be just equal to the current value of the output, a corresponding adjustment must be made in the measure of profits to eliminate those which arise from changes in the value of inventories rather than from changes in their physical volume. Inventory profits or losses occur when the cost, as recorded in the company's books, of goods removed from inventory differs from the current replacement cost of the goods.

The IVA is statistically the least reliable element in the estimation of NIPA corporate profits. The accuracy of the IVA depends on the extent and detail of the information about the inventory accounting methods used by corporations and on the reliability of the price indexes used to convert estimated book values to current replacement costs. As a later part of this study shows, little of the basic data input to the NIPA estimates of profits is obtained directly from corporate reports of profits; the basic data source is the Federal income tax return of several years preceding the year for which the NIPA estimate is made. To be sure, the inventory accounting method used by the corporation must be shown on its return, but if there is a widespread change in the method of inventory accounting between the most recent year for which tax return data are available and the current year, the NIPA estimating procedures are likely to fail to pick up this information. The magnitude of the resulting error depends on how extensive the shift in accounting was, the nature of the shift, and the magnitude of the change in the relevant price indices. The NIPA estimate of the IVA is highly suspect when, as in recent years, there is a rapid rise in the price level and an extensive shift from first-in, first-out (FIFO) to last-in, first-out (LIFO) book inventory accounting, which substantially accomplishes on company books the current replacement cost valuation of goods recovered from inventory.

Other adjustments are required to eliminate other valuation changes which, however appropriate they are for book and/or tax purposes, are inconsistent with the basic NIPA concept. Thus NIPA profits exclude capital gains and losses. While they include deductions for realized bad debts, they do not include deductions for additions to reserves for bad debts. State corporation income taxes are added back to the NIPA measure of before-tax profits. To avoid double counting, dividends received from domestic corporations are excluded from corporation receipts in determining profits (although dividends received from foreign corporations are included). Similarly, interest payments and receipts are netted out so that only the net amount received from or paid to the noncorporate sector is included in the reckoning of profits; net interest from abroad is included.

The NIPA measure the economy's total output on both a gross and net basis. Part of the total income flow generated by the economy's total production represents the exhaustion of existing physical production facilities. The net income and net output of the economy, therefore, must reflect that part of gross income and output which was used up in the production activity of the period. Only the consumption of reproducible production facilities, however, is taken into account; accordingly the exhaustion of natural resources — depletion — is not measured as an offset from gross production and gross income in arriving at net national product and national income.

The measure of capital consumption (CCA) charged against the total product of the corporate sector warrants special attention. Until recently, this measure was substantially the same, in concept and in measure, as depreciation allowed for tax purposes. Dissatisfaction with the latter for NIPA purposes was frequently expressed; the various accelerated methods allowed for computing depreciation and the "useful lives" which businesses are allowed to assign to depreciable facilities for tax purposes were deemed to result in depreciation allowances which did not accurately or consistently measure the real consumption of such facilities in a given period of time. As of the beginning of 1976, the BEA has presented new estimates of capital consumption. These estimates are no longer derived, as formerly, from tax return data; they are, instead, based on estimates of the stocks of fixed, depreciable capital and on a number of specific assumptions about the useful lives of physical production facilities and the annual rate of consumption of these facilities. For one thing, useful lives of equipment and nonresidential structures are assumed to be 85 percent of those listed in the 1942 edition of the (then) Bureau of Internal Revenue's Bulletin "F"; residential real property useful lives are assumed to be 80 years for new 1-to-4 unit dwellings and 65 years for new 5-or-more unit dwellings. These useful lives are materially longer than those allowed and, on the average, used by business for tax purposes. Moreover, the NIPA capital consumption allowances are estimated using only the straight-line method in which the annual depreciation equals the cost of the asset divided by the estimated useful life. These adjustments substantially reduce depreciation compared with the amounts reported on tax returns; to a lesser degree, they reduce NIPA capital consumption allowances below the amount of depreciation shown on company books. Finally, the NIPA estimate is based on current replacement cost rather then the original or historical cost of the existing stock of depreciable capital; current replacement cost is computed by applying the appropriate "implicit deflators for gross national product" to the original cost of each of the types of capital for each of the vintages of the existing capital.[6] This adjustment tends to increase NIPA capital consumption allowances above the amounts of depreciation for book and tax purposes. In the last few years, when the relevant price indexes rose sharply, this replacement cost adjustment has exceeded the adjustments to standardize depreciation accounting.

Book Profits

The measure of corporate profits in business accounting practice differs in a number of major respects from the NIPA measure, reflecting the difference in the purposes for which these measures are calculated. As computed by corporate financial officers, profits are more than a measure of the amount of the total income produced by the corporation which is claimed by its shareholders; as a percentage of the company's total assets and net worth, they are also a measure of the efficiency with which the company used the resources at its disposal during the period.

---

[6]Capital consumption allowances are also shown without these adjustments. The basic estimates of corporate profits shown in the NIPA since January 1976, however, are based on the adjusted capital consumption allowances. For a complete description of the conceptual content of the new capital consumption allowances and the adjustments thereto, see U.S. Department of Commerce, Bureau of Economic Analysis, *Survey of Current Business,* January 1976, Part I, pp. 3-7.

As such, profits are an essential indicator, to the corporation's management, to its shareholders, and to investors generally, of the effectiveness of the company's use of capital compared with that of other businesses, hence of the company's capacity to maintain and attract capital resources and of the real price it must pay for such resources.

The measure of profits for this purpose is the corporation's gross receipts attributable to the time period for which profits are to be measured, less all of the costs properly allocable to that time period which were incurred to produce the gross receipts. These charges are perceived as both monetary — i.e., costs for which money payments were made or liabilities incurred — and nonmonetary — i.e., costs which do not reflect payments, or liabilities for future payments, to specific persons. Examples of the first include wages and salaries, goods and services purchased from other businesses, interest payments, rental payments, insurance premiums, etc. The latter category includes allocations to reserves for bad debts, for depreciation, for depletion, and for future tax liabilities, amortization of goodwill and of investment in research and development, etc.

This highly abbreviated listing illustrates a number of the differences between book and NIPA profits which reflect the differences in the purposes for which profits are measured. For one thing, prudent financial management of a corporation requires that some of the current revenues be "set aside" — i.e., reserved from the amount of net income — to account for the possibility that some of the loans advanced by the company will not be fully repaid by the borrowers. In the NIPA, on the other hand, defaults on such loans do not affect the total amount of output produced nor the aggregate income claims therein; hence, charges to reserves for bad debts, reflecting business' estimates of future defaults, reducing profits, would have to be matched by a counter account showing additional income to debtors as a group. Insofar as these loans and the possible defaults thereupon are within the corporate sector, they would net out even if the attempt were made to measure the present value of the possible future defaults as income offsets to the lenders and income additions to the borrowers. To the extent that the loans are intersectoral with the corporate sector a net creditor, treating annual additions to a reserve for bad debts as a cost which reduces profits would require, as indicated, the allocation of an equal amount as additional income in the various components of the noncorporate sector. For the most part, the resulting reduction in corporate profits would show up as increases in business transfer payments, i.e., payments by business to persons for which the latter perform no current productive services.[7]

Another illustration of the conceptual differences attributable to differences in purpose is to be found in the treatment of depletion. As stated above, depletion is not treated as a charge against output in the NIPA since, by assumption, exhaustible natural resources cannot be replaced from current production. For any one corporation, however, failure to measure this exhaustion and to set its monetary value as a reservation of revenues from profits would mislead the company's shareholders. Assuming that depletion is measured for book purposes in a reasonably realistic way, it shows the decrease during the period in the amount of a given class of the company's assets. Equivalently, it shows the portion of a prepaid expense which was incurred at some given earlier date but which is properly attributable as a charge against the current period's operating results. An equal part of the company's revenues is, in effect, a measure of the consumption of the corporation's depletable, non-reproducible assets. Without a charge against revenues for the period's depletion, the company's total assets and net worth, as well as its net income, would be overstated; this overstatement of assets and net worth would increase through time.

Depreciation affords a further example of the purpose-related differences in the measurement of profits in the NIPA and in corporate financial statements. In business accounting, depreciation is not a measurement of the capital used up; it is, instead, a method of allocating over the extended period during which durable production facilities are expected to contribute to production the expense previously incurred to acquire these facilities. In accounting terminology, "Depreciation . . . aims to distribute the cost or other basic value of tangible capital assets,

---

[7]On the other hand, bad debts incurred during the current period are deducted and are treated as a business transfer payment. This is because the NIPA measures personal consumption expenditures before deduction for consumers' defaults. A charge against this amount of GNP is required to assure equality between the value of total output and the claims thereto.

less salvage (if any), over the estimated useful life of the unit (which may be a group of assets) in a systematic and rational manner. *It is a process of allocation, not of valuation.*"[8] Depreciation, hence, is a means for converting an asset — the prepaid expense — to current expense, related in some given way to each period's operations. In business accounting, depreciation is a charge against revenues, corresponding to the reduction in the amount of existing depreciable assets which is needed to show net revenues; in these respects book depreciation and NIPA depreciation are similar in purpose. But the purpose of book depreciation does not extend further to showing how much of the company's revenues must be set aside to maintain the production capacity on hand at the beginning of the accounting period, although with appropriate adjustments for changes in replacement costs, the current year's depreciation charge may be so interpreted.[9] Accordingly, the basis for computing the company's depreciation is the original cost of the facilities, not their reproduction or replacement costs.

In view of these differences in purpose and the diversity of operations among corporations, business accounting should be expected to result in substantial differences from one company to another in the amount of annual depreciation with respect to equal amounts of depreciable facilities. This expectation appears to be reasonable even where substantially similar facilities are involved. Taking account of the differences in the types of facilities used by different companies and of the differences in the specialization of their use only reinforces the view that variation rather than uniformity in annual rates of depreciation from one company to another is the rule rather than the exception. Profits as measured for book purposes, accordingly, should be expected to reflect the various elements of diversity which will affect each company's measure of depreciation.

---

[8]American Institute of Certified Public Accountants, *Accounting Research and Terminology Bullets — Final Edition,* (New York: AICPA, 1961). Emphasis added.

---

[9]Indeed, during periods of substantial change in the general level of prices some such adjustments may be highly useful in providing information regarding the company's real growth (positive or negative).

Given its purpose in business accounting, the amount of depreciation in a given period depends on expectations as to how long the facility (or facilities) will prove to be economically useful to the company (not how long the facility will be physically capable of contributing to the output of any one company — or succession of companies). It also depends on the pattern through time of its expected contribution to the company's output. Neither of these determinations can be rigorously made. In large part, each is based on the company's past experience, modified, perhaps, by factors which are expected to differ from those in the past. Depreciation accounting for book purposes, accordingly, tends to follow conventions rather than seeking to determine precisely the "actual" conversion of prepaid to current expense in each accounting period.

For NIPA purposes, on the other hand, this particularization of depreciation to each company is irrelevant. The economic life of a facility in the hands of any one company is likely often to be less than its full life when account is taken of its transfer by sale or other disposition to another company or to a succession of companies. It is the full life which, presumably, should be the base for computing NIPA capital consumption allowances. Similarly, the pattern of depreciation through time for any one company with respect to an asset or group of assets, while perfectly appropriate to the company, is likely to differ from the time distribution of depreciation when account is taken, as in the NIPA concept, of a succession of users of the property or properties. Hence, conceptual differences are likely, *in the abstract,* to produce differing estimates of depreciation for a given stock of facilities.

Another major difference between NIPA and business accounting measures of profits, reflecting differences in the purposes served by the respective measures, concerns capital gains and losses. While these cannot enter into the NIPA measure, which identifies profits as one of the charges or income claims on the value of current output, they cannot be excluded from the measure of any one corporation's profits. While the gains or losses realized by a company as a result of its disposition of some of its assets may not be a major focus of its operations, such gains or losses nonetheless alter the amount of its total assets and net worth. Excluding them from the company's profits would make it impossible to reconcile the company's beginning-of-the-year and its end-of-year balance sheets.

A number of other obvious differences between book and NIPA profit measures are also attributable to differences in objectives. For example, there clearly is no reason for any one company to exclude dividend or interest receipts from its revenues for book purposes, even though this exclusion is entirely appropriate for the NIPA.

Profits for Tax Purposes

Profits as measured for income tax purposes differ from both the NIPA and book concepts in numerous respects. Here, too, the differences do not reflect conceptual deficiencies in one or another measure but differences in the purposes for which profits are measured. To be sure, profits for tax purposes do suffer from major conceptual disabilities, resulting in disproportionately heavy tax burdens on the returns to corporate equity, thereby severely aggravating the basic income tax bias against private saving and capital formation.[10] Amelioration of this disproportionately heavy burden would require substantial modification of the present tax measure of profits, substantially increasing the difference between this measure and both the book and NIPA measures. Notwithstanding, the existing differences principally reflect a significant number of specific public policy objectives the achievement of which were sought by differentially specifying the way in which various receipts and expenditures or costs should be taken into account for tax purposes. To repeat the observation made frequently above, the concept and measure of profits for tax purposes is not to be faulted because it differs from other concepts and measures; they are to be criticized, instead, with respect to their failure to conform with the appropriate criteria of taxation.

The large number and variety of tax provisions which differentially affect the tax, book, and NIPA measures of corporate profits precludes any comprehensive listing and discussion of these differences in this

---

[10]For an extended and detailed discussion, cf Norman B. Ture and B. Kenneth Sanden, *The Effects of Tax Policy on Capital Formation,* Financial Executives Research Foundation, (New York, 1977).

study. One of the principal differences concerns the tax treatment of capital gains and losses, excluded from the NIPA measure and fully included, in the general case, for book purposes. In brief summary of a complex set of provisions, a company's capital gains may be excluded from its profits for ordinary tax purposes, and taxed separately at a lower rate. However, some gains, treated as capital gains for tax purposes, are treated as ordinary income in the NIPA and book measures.

In recent years, one of the quantiatively most important items contributing to the differences among tax, book, and NIPA measures of profits is the income of U.S. corporations' foreign branches and the equity interest of the branches in foreign corporations. For the calendar year 1972, for example, the NIPA adjustment of tax return data with respect to this item amounted to about $9.5 billion, 9.9 percent of the NIPA measure of "corporate profits before tax" and 10.3 percent of the NIPA measure of corporate profits. Under the generally applicable provisions of the income tax, dividends, irrespective of source, are not included in a shareholder's income until received from the paying corporation. This applies to corporate shareholders in foreign subsidiaries as well as to individual shareholders in domestic corporations. When these dividends from foreign subsidiaries are received, they are grossed up by the amount of foreign income and excess profits taxes paid or deemed to have been paid; this gross-up is allowed as a credit (subject to certain limitations) against the U.S. income tax liability on the grossed-up amount. On the other hand, U.S. corporations operating branches abroad, as distinct from those holding an equity interest in foreign corporations, must include branch income in their taxable income in the year in which the income is earned, irrespective of whether the foreign income is remitted by the branch to the U.S. company. In general business accounting practice, U.S. companies with foreign branches and subsidiaries consolidate all of their pretax foreign earnings or losses with domestic earnings in determining pretax profits for book purposes. The NIPA measure of profits eliminates foreign earnings as reported on corporate tax returns and replaces this measure with a measure of foreign earnings of U.S. corporations that is consistent with the definitions in the balance of payments accounts. The resulting NIPA measure is income, gross of foreign income taxes, on equities in foreign corporations received by all U.S. residents, net of correspending outflow. The NIPA measure, thus, differs materially from both the tax return and book measures.

Depreciation as measured for tax purposes often differs materially in concept from both book and NIPA measures. These differences result from several component elements in the calculation of depreciation which in recent years have tended to be substantially offsetting. In 1972, for example, the tax return measure of corporations' depreciation allowances was about $0.7 billion, or one percent, less than the NIPA measure. But the near equality in these measures results from very large differences in the measure of the factors which determine the amount of depreciation. For example, the NIPA adjustment to put tax return depreciation on a current replacement cost rather than historical cost basis added $12.9 billion to the tax-return amount, while the NIPA adjustment to put tax return depreciation on a straight-line basis, using substantially longer "useful lives," subtracted $15.4 billion (other, smaller adjustments for conceptual differences make up the difference between the $2.5 billion net subtraction with respect to these two items and the $0.7 billion addition overall.)

Any comparison of book with tax return or NIPA depreciation should not be construed as suggesting that any of the three measures of depreciation is "wrong" in some general sense. Each measure serves its own appropriate and legitimate purpose and should be evaluated only in terms of its particular purpose and the criteria relevant thereto. The differences between the tax and other measures are attributable primarily to the use for tax purposes of shorter useful lives and accelerated depreciation formulae. Contrary to popular assertion, this does not mean that tax depreciation is "unrealistic." One of the basic canons of taxation is that taxes should be neutral. Tax neutrality is not always rigorously defined, but its principal significance is that a tax system — or features thereof — should not alter the *relative* prices which private sector entities, households and businesses, confront. Among other things, this means that the tax system should not increase the cost of saving uses of income or capital formation uses of production capability disproportinately with the cost of consumption. To satisfy this criterion, an income tax must either allow an immediate deduction for current saving (or equivalently, capital outlays) or exclude the returns thereupon from the tax base.[11] Depreciation provisions, no matter how short the useful lives or how accelerated the formula, fail to meet this test in that the deduction is delayed over some time period rather than being allowed at the time of the expenditure.

Expensing of capital outlays, rather than depreciation, is called for by the tax neutrality criterion. It does not follow, obviously, that expensing is also called for in the NIPA or in the calculation of profits for book purposes. By the same token, it does not follow that tax depreciation is "unrealistic" because it doesn't conform with book or NIPA measures.

Depletion allowed for tax purposes differs from that generally measured for book purposes; as already noted, depletion is not treated as a charge against revenues for estimating profits in the NIPA. For tax purposes, a company may compute its depletion allowance either by use of the adjusted basis method (i.e., cost depletion) or as a stipulated percentage of the gross income, but not to exceed 50 percent of the net income, obtained from the mineral property. For the most part, depletion for book purposes is computed as an allocation of the investment in the property over its estimated producing life. As in the case of depreciation, the differences in the methods of computation for book and tax purposes — and the effects of these differences on measured profits — do not imply that one is correct and the other wrong. They reflect, instead, the differences in the purposes for which each is intended.

Apart from the NIPA adjustment to put capital consumption allowances on a current replacement rather than historical cost basis, the differences among NIPA, book, and tax measures of depreciation and depletion largely reflect differences in timing. Timing differences account for a number of other differences in measured profits. Principal among these are instalment sales. For book purposes, such sales — and the equivalent purchases — are customarily treated as generating an equal amount of revenues in the period in which the sales are made, even though cash receipts — or disbursements — will extend over a longer period of time. For tax purposes, however, the receipts need be taken

---

[11]For a proof of this proposition, cf. Ture and Sanden, op. cit. pp.

into revenues only as they are realized. The rapidly rising trend of instalment sales and instalment credit outstanding would tend to increase the divergences between sales revenues as measured for book and tax purposes. Moreover, irregularities in the growth of instalment sales over time makes meaningful comparison of book and tax sales revenues in any one period extremely difficult, requiring a highly detailed analysis and time distribution of the instalment sales contracts outstanding in the period. The NIPA profits measure attempts to adjust for this timing difference, but these adjustments are based on highly fragmentary information. It is likely, therefore, that the NIPA profits measure more closely reflects the tax treatment than the book treatment of instalment sales, although conceptually NIPA treatment should conform with book treatment.

Table I illustrates some of the major differences in the book, tax, and NIPA treatment of various income and expense items in the determination of profits. A hypothetical corporation, the XYZ Co., engages in the manufacture of consumer durables and business capital goods. Its sales are made on both a cash and credit basis; it elects to account for instalment sales on a cash basis for tax — but not for book — purposes. The company uses the straight-line method for book depreciation and accelerated depreciation methods for tax purposes. For both book and tax purposes, it accounts for inventories on a FIFO basis. It operates a foreign branch and wholly-owned domestic and foreign mining subsidiaries. It has investments in the common stocks and bonds of a number of domestic U.S. corporations. The company operates a funded pension plan for its employees and a deferred compensation plan for certain of its executives.

TABLE I. Book, Tax, and NIPA Profit Measurement

	Book (000)	Tax (000)	NIPA (000)
Sales and Other Revenues			
Net sales (instalments sales = $1,000,000; payments received on instalment sales = $700,000)	$15,115	$14,815	$15,115
Interest income (interest received from corporate borrowers = $75,000; interest received from noncorporate borrowers = $125,000)	200	200	125
Capital gains	10	10	—
Dividends received on common stock investments	300	45	—
Total revenue from domestic sources	15,625	15,070	15,240
Costs and Expenses			
Costs of goods sold	9,375	9,375	9,375
Inventory valuation adjustment	—	—	75
Selling and administration	1,250	1,250	1,250
Wages and salaries not included above	900	900	900
Employee benefits, including payroll taxes (reserved for future deferred compensation = $75,000; deferred compensation paid = $25,000)	740	690	690
Interest (interest paid to corporate lenders = $400,000; interest paid to noncorporate lenders = $200,000)	600	600	200
Bad debts			
Allocated to reserve	100	100	—
Current losses	—	—	85
Depreciation	400	460	380
Capital consumption adjustment	—	—	48

	Book (000)	Tax (000)	NIPA (000)
Depletion	45	60	—
Mine development expenditures	40	300	40
State and local taxes			
Income	87	87	—
Property and other	160	160	160
Total costs and expenses	13,697	13,982	13,203
Domestic Earnings	1,928	1,118	2,037
Pretax Earnings of Foreign Subsidiaries and Branches (branch earnings = \$260; subsidiary earnings = 265; dividends paid to U.S. parent = \$70)	525	395	70
Total earnings	2,453	1,513	2,107
Federal Income Tax:			
Preliminary tax		709	
Less: Foreign tax credit		245	
Investment tax credit		100	
Federal income tax liability	364	364	364
State and local income taxes	—	—	87
Foreign income taxes	245	245	—
Total	609	609	451
After-tax Earnings	1,844	904	1,656

Procedures for Estimating Corporate Profits in the NIPA

This discussion has been at pains to show major differences in the concepts and measures of profits among NIPA, book, and tax accounting, arguing that these differences derive from differences in the purposes for which profits are measured. Revisions in the NIPA estimates of corporate profits for a given year or years cannot properly be construed as reflecting poor quality in business accounting practice and in the financial reports corporations provide their shareholders unless the NIPA revisions were impelled by changes in the book measures of profits for the same years. This is not the case. NIPA profits estimates are based primarily on tax return data, not directly on book data. Revisions of financial statements to shareholders are inputs to revisions of NIPA estimates only insofar as they require revisions of tax returns. To be sure, this sequence of revisions can occur and probably does, to some limited extent.[12] But revisions of preliminary projections to take account of tax return tabulations are far more generally the initial link in the chain, with greater effects on NIPA estimates than on the corporation's books of accounts.

The following discussion details the NIPA estimating procedures and delineates the linkage to corporate tax returns. It also examines the revisions in the NIPA measures. The conclusion which emerges from this examination is that the NIPA estimating procedures themselves are principally responsible for the revisions, large and small, that characterize this data output. To repeat, these revisions do not reflect inadequacies in business accounting practice.

Estimates of corporate profits in the NIPA are prepared by the Bureau of Economic Analysis (BEA) in the U.S. Department of Commerce. BEA has followed substantially the same procedures in estimating corporate profits for approximately a quarter of a century. To assure clarity, this exposition will detail specifically the estimation of 1976 corporate profits and the concurrent refinement of prior years'

---

[12]According to the Bureau of Economic Analysis, the average revision in the basic tax return item used in the NIPA estimate of profits averaged only 0.6 percent for the years 1963-72.

profit estimates, the results of which appeared in the July, 1977 issue of the *Survey of Current Business*

The Internal Revenue Service is BEA's primary source of data for estimating corporate profits, both by industry and in the aggregate, because every corporation is required to file a tax return on an annual basis and is subject to IRS audit.[13] IRS statistical compilations of tax return data for any given year, however, are not available in complete form until two or more years after the taxable year for which the tax returns are filed. Hence, BEA uses a number of procedures to bring forward in time an earlier IRS estimate as the basis for a more recent year's NIPA estimate of corporate profits.

To make the "initial" estimate of 1976 corporate profits,[14] BEA begins with a benchmark or "final" estimate of 1974 corporate profits by two-digit industry, using IRS estimates of net income on tax returns (labeled "total receipts less total deductions" in *Statistics of Income . . . 1974 Corporation Income Tax Returns*"). These estimates are then subjected to a series of conceptual adjustments in order to reconcile profits reported for tax purposes with the concept of profits employed

---

[13]The tax return data are obtained by IRS from samples, not from a census, of corporate tax returns. The magnitude of the sampling variability depends on the sampling rate which varies directly with the size of the corporation. Differences in these sampling rates are reflected in differences in sampling variability for any given receipt or deduction among industry divisions and among receipts and deductions within any given industry.

---

[14]The word "initial" is set in quotation marks in recognition of the fact that the July 1977 estimate to which it refers is not literally the first published estimate of 1976 profits. This appears in the January 1977 issue of the *Survey of Current Business* and in each of the subsequent issues, often revised twice or more before the July estimate These pre-July estimates rely on the technique used for making quarterly estimates, described below at p. 28. The January estimate is based on estimates of profits for the first three quarters of the year plus a fourth quarter "implicit" estimate which is derived as a residual by using the preliminary fourth quarter estimate of GNP, assuming the last quarter's statistical discrepancy is the same as the third quarter's. The first three quarters' profits estimates for 1976 are extrapolations based on preliminary tabulations of IRS returns for 1974. Another estimate is presented in March, based on extrapolations of 1974 IRS tabulations for four quarters of 1976. Hereafter, except as noted, the word initial, without quotation marks, will be used to mean the July estimate.

in the NIPA. The major adjustments include adding to IRS net income the profits expected to be disclosed by audit, the income of Federal Reserve Banks and two Federal agencies, and three items originally deducted from gross receipts on tax returns: State income taxes, the bad debt adjustment, and depletion allowances. Deducted from IRS estimates are reported capital gains and dividends received from domestic corporations. Finally, remittances from abroad are substituted for foreign earnings. The profits of two-digit industry groups are then summed to find aggregate corporate profits for the year.

In addition to being used in computing 1976 estimates, these benchmarks of 1974 corporate profits for each industry and in the aggregate are published as BEA's "final" estimates of the incorporated business sector's profits for that year — 1974. While published as final, this year's, that is 1977's, estimate of 1974 corporate profits will be subject to change at the time of the next major revision of the NIPA. In the past, these revisions as discussed below, have entailed either or both statistical and conceptual changes in the various components of the NIPA. As a consequence, this year's "final" estimate of 1974 corporate profits may never be absolutely final since, as has been the case frequently in the past, future revisions may alter the definition of profits used in the NIPA, hence may necessitate changes in the values of any given, or all, earlier years' estimates.

The second stage in the process of estimating 1976's profits in the NIPA involves making the same conceptual adjustments to preliminary and incomplete 1975 tax-return data by industry and summing to obtain aggregate corporate profits. After being checked for consistency against the 1974 benchmark estimates of profits, which are fully adjusted conceptually to the NIPA concept of profits, these benchmark approximations are substituted in the NIPA for the last published, i.e., the intial estimates of 1975 corporate profits. These approximations of 1975 profits then become a primary input to the third stage of the process of estimating 1976 profits.

This third stage proceeds by extrapolating the 1975 benchmark approximations of industry profits to 1976 by reference to the relationship between 1976 and 1975 corporate pretax *book* profits shown in financial reports submitted to the Federal Trade Commission or other regulatory agencies or by some other indicator of business activity. If these extrapolators indicate, say, a 30 percent increase in 1976's corporate book profits over 1975's, the benchmark approximations of 1975's NIPA profits are increased 30 percent to find 1976's initial estimate. The extrapolator series for different industries vary in reliability and content and may be changed periodically when improved data sources or statistical and sampling techniques become available. Extrapolators are applied to industry benchmark approximations. No conceptual adjustments are made to preliminary profits estimates; rather, past relationships between NIPA and other measures of profits are assumed to be constant and extrapolated forward. Once the extrapolations of profits are completed, the resulting estimates will be published in the NIPA as preliminary, first-year estimates of corporate profits for 1976.

In 1978, BEA will publish a second-year estimate of 1976 corporate profits. This estimate, referred to as the benchmark approximation, is based on preliminary IRS tabulations of 1976 tax returns. The final, third-year estimate of 1976 corporate profits, based on final — benchmark — IRS data, will be included in the NIPA in July of 1979. Figure 1 describes the procedures for the successive estimates of 1976's corporate profits.

BEA will also make available quarterly estimates of corporate profits for the current year, 1977. These are prepared by interpolating within the annual estimates for prior years, using the same series employed to extrapolate the second-year benchmark approximations beyond the years for which IRS data are available. These interpolating series are then used to extrapolate quarterly estimates into the most current calendar year. Since samples of publicly-reporting companies are either unavailable or considerably smaller on a quarterly basis and since these estimates must initially be seasonally adjusted and ultimately reconciled with annual estimates, when made, the quarterly estimates are much less accurate than are any of the subsequent annual estimates of profits.

Variability in NIPA Estimates of Corporate Profits

The accuracy of the data used in estimating profits, hence the reliability of any one estimate of a given year's profits, diminishes the more recent the period for which the estimate is made; in reverse order of accuracy, quarterly and preliminary first-year estimates are less

Figure 1. BEA's Procedure for Estimating 1976 Corporate Profits

Preliminary (July 1977) Estimate			2nd Year (July 1978) Estimate		3rd Year (July 1979) Estimate
Stage 1	Stage 2	Stage 3	Stage 1	Stage 2	—
A. Tabulate "final" IRS data on 1974 tax return profits by industry	A. Tabulate preliminary IRS data on 1975 tax return profits by industry	A. Determine approximate 1976 profits from financial statements or other indices of business activity	A. Tabulate "final" IRS data on 1975 tax return profits by industry	A. Tabulate preliminary IRS data on 1976 tax return profits by industry	A. Tabulate "final" IRS data on 1976 tax return profits by industry
B. Adjust 1974 taxable income to NIPA conceptual basis to find benchmark estimate of 1974 corporate profits	B. Adjust 1975 taxable income to NIPA conceptual basis to find benchmark approximation of 1975 corporate profits	B. Create ratio of 1976 to 1975 approximations from same sources	B. Adjust 1975 taxable income to NIPA conceptual basis to find benchmark estimate of 1975 profits	B. Adjust 1976 taxable income to NIPA conceptual basis to find benchmark approximation of 1976 corporate profits	B. Adjust 1976 taxable income to NIPA conceptual basis
	C. Benchmark approximation of 1975 corporate profits checked for consistency with 1974 benchmark from Stage 1	C. Benchmark approximation of 1975 corporate profits is multiplied by ratios to find 1976 preliminary estimate		C. Benchmark approximation checked for consistency with 1975 benchmark from Stage 1	
Published July of 1977 as final estimate of 1974 corporate profits	Published July 1977 as preliminary second-year estimate of 1975 corporate profits	Published July 1977 as preliminary first-year estimate of 1976 corporate profits	Published July 1978 as final estimate of 1975 corporate profits	Published July of 1979 preliminary second-year estimate of 1976 profits	Published July 1978 as as "final" estimate of 1976 corporate profits

reliable than second year estimates and, despite persistent errors in some industry divisions, third-year estimates are yet more accurate. In general, the industry extrapolations have been far less accurate than their sum since errors in one industry have tended to offset errors in others. The differential error among industries results from the facts that (1) comprehensive and timely data for building the extrapolator series are not avaiable for all industries, (2) the rate of change in corporate profits cannot be estimated in all instances from samples of current profits data, and (3) there are shifts in the industry classification of multi-product corporations.

The major industries in the NIPA are Agriculture, Forestry, and Fisheries; Mining; Contract Construction; Manufacturing; Transportation; Communication; Electric, Gas, and Sanitary Services; Wholesale and Retail Trade; Finance, Insurance, and Real Estate; Services; and Rest of the World. Of these, manufacturing is the largest, accounting for one-third to one-half of the total profits in the years 1947 through 1973, followed by finance, insurance, and real estate, comprising 10% to 25% of the total, and wholesale and retail trade which totals 10% to 20%.

Since the third-year benchmark estimates of corporate profits by industry are based on completed IRS tabulations of tax returns, hence on IRS's sample of the entire universe, the absolute value of the percentage difference between these final NIPA estimates and preliminary first-year estimates of profits provides a measure of the accuracy of BEA's estimation procedures. The difference in successive estimates of profits by industry were computed for the period, 1948-72. Table II presents the arithmetic means, or averages, of these percentage differences, by major industries; for purposes of these tabulations communications has been grouped with electric, gas, and sanitary services (referred to hereafter as utilities).[15]

---

[15]In this and following tables, the numbers refer to the NIPA measure of corporate profits before tax rather than to corporate profits with inventory valuation and capital consumption adjustments. The latter adjustment was not made in the NIPA estimates until 1976. The former adjustment is not made for three industries, Agriculture, Finance and Services. Corporate profits before tax is a more nearly consistent measure, therefore, through time and cross sectionally.

As the table shows, the average change from the first to the third estimates for communications and utilities is smaller than that for aggregate corporate profits, while the average change for manufacturing only slightly exceeds that for the aggregate. Those for the other industries are substantially larger; in the case of contract construction, for example, the change averages almost one-fourth of the "final" estimate. It is also interesting to note that the larger the average change between the first and third estimates, the smaller the relative change between the second and third estimates.

TABLE II. Before-Tax Corporate Profits Estimates by Industry; Mean of the Annual Percentage Changes, 1948-1972

	Mean Change (%)	
	1st Year Preliminary to 2nd Year Estimate	*1st Year to 3rd Year Estimate*
Aggregate Corporate Profits	2.5	4.4
Industry:		
Manufacturing	2.9	4.5
Communications and Utilities	2.6	3.3
Wholesale and Retail Trade	7.3	8.9
Finance, Insurance, & Real Estate	5.2	6.8
Services	13.4	14.1
Mining	17.8	19.4
Transportation	23.0	21.5
Contract Construction	19.8	26.6

Source: U.S Department of Commerce, *Survey of Current Business,* National Income Issues.

Note: The measures were computed as the sum of the percentage differences, disregarding the sign, between the initial and the benchmark approximation estimates and the initial and final benchmark estimates for each of the calendar years, divided by the number of years for which these estimates were available.

The reasons for such enormous differences in accuracy among the industries' profits estimates can largely be traced to several characteristics of the source data used to construct the extrapolator series for each major industry. The data vary in terms of their definitional comparability with BEA's concept of profits and in the coverage and representativeness of the samples from which they are derived. Both discrepancies affect the level and movement of the extrapolator series and result in errors in the estimates based on them. Moreover, for some industries, no current profit data are available; hence the extrapolators must be based on sales data adjusted by estimated profit margins or on some other indicator of change in business activity. Industry estimates based on the latter type of extrapolator series invariably exhibit the largest errors when measured against the benchmark estimate of profits; as will be shown in a later discussion, some portion of the errors for certain industries frequently remains uncorrected until the NIPA undergo major revision. Critical to an evaluation of the reliability of the NIPA corporate sector, therefore, is a thorough understanding of BEA's procedures for constructing these indicators of the rate of change in industry profits.

The data used by BEA for estimating the rate of change in manufacturing profits is obtained from the Federal Trade Commission's sample data published in the *Quarterly Financial Report* (QFR). This is BEA's most important source of information for obtaining the extrapolators discussed above; it has been used for this purpose since 1947 and more recently for mining and the wholesale and retail trade industries. QFR data is based on regular reports from approximately 11,000 manufacturing corporations, sampled from a universe of over 200,000 which are required to file financial statements with the Securities and Exchange Commission either because they are listed on a securities exchange or otherwise registered. The FTC also adjusts for the incidence of nonreporting each period.

The sample of manufacturing corporations is a composite drawn from two mutually exclusive sampling frames to insure comprehensive, up-to-date coverage; the IRS file of those companies required to file form 1120 or 1120-S is sampled once a year and the Social Security Administration's file of applications for employer identification numbers is drawn from each quarter. The sample is stratified and expanded in terms of asset-size classes. Virtually all manufacturing corporations with assets greater than $10 million are permanent sample members; in the sample for the third quarter of 1976, these companies were 66.4 percent of the total sample. For those in smaller asset classes, the fraction varies. Approximately 5.7 percent of the universe of manufacturing corporations was included in the survey in that quarter. Once selected a corporation is legally bound to comply with survey procedures.

Companies selected for the FTC sample are required to provide the financial data called for in the FTC questionnaire within 25 days after the close of each calendar quarter. The data so supplied, obviously, are preliminary; moreover, no revisions are required by FTC of the sampled companies. Nonetheless, these data appear to afford a consistent and reliable basis for estimating changes in profits.

The financial data recorded in the *Quarterly Financial Reports* embody the accounting conventions adopted generally for financial reporting purposes, that is, the book concept of profits. While this measure of profits differs from both the tax and NIPA concepts, in many important respects *QFR* data afford a more consistent, hence better basis for estimating changes in profits (and its determinant components) than do tax data.

Data on profits for industries subject to regulation, e.g., banking and securities, communications, public utilities, and transportation, are from the financial statements which companies in these industries are legally required to submit to their respective regulatory agencies — the Federal Deposit Insurance Corporation, Federal Power Commission, the Interstate Commerce Commission, and Civil Aeronautics Board. The coverage of data used in extrapolation is nearly complete, and the data are required on a timely basis. Except for a few cases, most notably the transportation industry, the profits data submitted from corporation reports conform closely with standard business accounting concepts. Accordingly, they provide a conceptually more consistent basis than do tax data for estimating changes in corporate financial items. The extrapolator series for transportation industries are derived from a variety of sources. Airline data come from reports filed with CAB. Railroad and motor freight data are taken directly from financial reports submitted to the ICC; however, the conceptual differences between profits reported to this regulatory agency and the IRS are much more significant than in the case of other regulated industries. Depreciation for "rehabilitation" capital expenditures by the railroads exemplifies the estimation problem. For regulatory and tax purposes, the railroads are permitted immediate expensing whereas normally a corporation would capitalize the initial outlay and depreciate this amount over some estimated "useful life." The amounts involved are substantial; in 1976, Conrail wrote off $230 million. Since BEA receives totals rather than depreciation by type of expenditure, the required adjustment to the NIPA basis is difficult prior to the benchmark IRS year.

Profits for motor freight are estimated from a poorly controlled sample of the largest companies. This industry has a very fluid population and a relatively large proportion of small and closely-held corporations; the sample which is used as an indicator of direction of change in profits, therefore, is extremely unrepresentative. Profits of several other sub-industries, for example, water transport and pipeline companies, are extrapolated using sales data which lag the initial estimates. Consolidated reporting by diversified companies may account for a portion of the error in the aggregate industry estimates.

Wholesale and retail trade profits, since the third quarter of 1974, have been extrapolated using FTC data. The FTC sample characteristics for these industries are essentially the same as for manufacturing, although the fraction of all firms surveyed is considerably smaller. From the 350,000 retail corporations, stratified by asset-size class, 2,113 are sampled; of this number, 596, or 28 percent fall in the over $10 million class and are permanent sample members. Among the approximately 170,000 wholesale corporations filing with the IRS, 2,812 are actually sampled; 1,155 of the wholesale sample report assets exceeding $10 million. Far more retail and wholesale corporations than manufacturing corporations are closely held and/or relatively small, and a large proportion of trade corporations — 54½ percent in 1974 — file their tax returns as small business corporations. Since 1120S corporations use more specialized systems of accounts and different terminology and since smaller corporations lack sophisticated accounting systems, a more significant bias may be present in these industries' profits data reported in *QFR*. Nevertheless, the financial data are taken directly from corporate reports to shareholders and, as is true of manufacturing, are more consistent and more closely conform with business accounting concepts than do IRS tax return data. They are, therefore, a more reliable data set for the extrapolators used by BEA.

Prior to 1974, and throughout the period studied here, retail and wholesale trade industries' profits were extrapolated using data from other sources. Like several other industries which are covered neither by the QFR series nor by reports to regulatory agencies, retail trade estimates were extrapolated from data published in Moody's *Manual of Industrial Securities,* drawn from published financial reports of individual companies. Profits, dividends, and taxes were compiled by line of trade for corporations accounting for 4/5 of retail profits. The remainder was extrapolated by references to sales data adjusted for changes in profit margins. The coverage of data in *Industrial Securities* is, however, less adequate than that from *QFR* or regulatory agencies, and for most industries the sample reported is less representative, including only the largest corporations.

Wholesale corporations' profits were extrapolated using estimates of the gross sales of merchant-wholesalers, obtained from the Bureau of the Census, and making an allowance for probable changes in profit-sales ratios. A base period estimate of this radio was taken from IRS benchmark data and adjusted by reference to various indicators including the corresponding ratio for retail trade from Moody's. Throughout the period 1948-72, estimates of wholesale profits were far less accurate than those for the retail industry.

It seems reasonable to assume that estimates of wholesale and retail corporations' profits will be more reliable in the future as a consequence of the comprehensiveness of FTC sampling procedures. However, since NIPA corporate profits estimates for 1974 and 1975 were pre-empted by the 1976 major revision, this speculation may not be tested for some time.

Extrapolation of the finance, insurance, and real estate corporate profits is based on sample data compiled by the SEC and FDIC for securities companies, by the Federal Reserve Board for banks, by the

Institute of Life Insurance for insurance corporations and the Insurance Information Institute, and by the Federal Savings and Loan Insurance Corporation for the real estate industry. Regulatory agencies provide fairly complete aggregates for financial corporations which do not differ substantially in coverage from the NIPA estimates. Profits estimates for the insurance industry are less reliable, since they are based on extrapolations of sales data from the ILI's "insurance written" series rather than on corporate financial reports. The tabulations of sample data on real estate corporations' sales and profit margins are less representative, hence extrapolation errors have been more frequent, than for the insurance industry and others estimated using similar data.

There are available only scanty if any current data on profits for the service sector. In general, base year IRS data are extrapolated with indicators of total sales and adjusted by historical profit margins or with nonsales indicators of gross business volume such as payroll data. When the latter procedure is necessary, profit ratios are frequently estimated by means of regressions of profits against historical measures of these indicators. Total sales indicators and consequently profits estimates have improved through time as the requisite information on different industries became available from reliable private sources, such as trade organizations. BEA also recently instituted in-house surveys.

Mining and contract construction corporations' profits estimates have been highly erratic throughout the period. Until 1974, extrapolations of mining profits were derived from sample data tabulated by private organizations; while the sample was not inordinately small, many mining corporations are closely-held or subsidiaries of corporations in other industries, and those which report financial results use specialized systems of accounts. BEA now compiles and tabulates data from a sample of mining companies. Contract construction is estimated from a limited annual sample administered by BEA. Benchmark IRS data are extrapolated by applying this estimate of the monetary value of construction activity adjusted by a constant profit margin. Estimates for these corporations have been very erratic; however, since the industry is composed of numerous and changing small companies, a more extensive sample would be costly.

Finally, the agriculture, forestry and fisheries industry and the rest-of-world component are estimated using Department of Agriculture data and BEA's balance of payments division's quarterly survey, respectively. (These were excluded from Table II.)

It should be obvious from this review of BEA's estimation procedures that corporate accounting and reporting practices are not responsible for the often substantial changes in BEA's estimates of corporate profits. Corporate financial statements do not provide the basic data for the NIPA estimates; the data base, as shown, is the IRS sample of corporate tax returns. Corporate financial statements provide, instead, the source for estimating changes in profits in the estimation periods for which tax return data are not available.

Profits data drawn from corporate financial statements have the advantage of a high degree of conceptual consistency from period to period. Even when obtained on a preliminary basis, they afford highly reliable measures of changes in profits even if the data ultimately supplied by corporations to their shareholders, regulatory agencies, and the public show different absolute amounts of profits. Indeed, if industries are catalogued on the basis of the source of materials for construction of the extrapolator series used to extend IRS benchmark data, those for which the extrapolators are obtained directly from corporate financial reports consistently exhibit the smallest changes in the NIPA profits estimates. Three separate groups of industries would emerge on this classification scheme for the years under study. The first group consists of manufacturing and the regulated industries, including communications and utilities (but not including transportation), for which profits recorded in corporate financial reports serve directly as extrapolators. The second most reliable estimates are found in the industrial classifications where both financial reports and adequate sales data are the bases for extrapolation; in this case, the more erratic profits estimates of a few sub-industries produced by reliance on sales and profit margin data are partially compensated. This group includes finance, insurance, and real estate, and the wholesale and retail trade industries. Mining must also be included, but as detailed above, the sample for this industry has been nonrepresentative, hence biased. The service and contract construction industries, extrapolated by frequently inadequate sales data or other indicators of business volume, make up the third group. While contributing a fairly small fraction of total profits, its extremely large errors have influenced the accuracy of aggregate profits estimates.

Table III shows, for each year 1948-72, the percentage difference between the preliminary and benchmark estimates of selected industries' profits; industries were selected to be representative of the three groupings described above. The table is constructed to show the percentage by which first estimates of each industry's profits deviate from what is assumed to be final, that is, from 1.00. Industries are ordered from left to right in terms of the magnitude of the percentage change from first to final estimates. Estimates for the manufacturing and communications and utilities industries, using financial statement data for extrapolation, outperform the other three; finance, insurance, and real estate estimates, while exhibiting the largest number of "perfect" estimates, are more erratic because of periodic biases in the samples of sales data and non-representative profit/sales margins for real estate and insurance companies; contract construction, for which estimates are extrapolated with insufficient surveys of gross output in the industry, is noticeably more erratic. For the entire period, communications and utilities estimates are as reliable as those for aggregate profits.

In the light of the estimation procedures described above, it is difficult to perceive how the magnitude of NIPA changes from first to final estimates of corporate profits can be meaningfully associated with changes in the quality of accounting for book purposes. To establish any such association, it would be necessary to show that changes in book accounting concepts and procedures coincide in time with the years for which NIPA preliminary estimates diverge most substantially from final estimates and to explain how and why these changes affect the reliability of estimates, obtained from corporate financial statements, of year-to-year changes in book profits. To be sure, the concepts and procedures used by the accounting profession are not static; as in the case of any other profession, there is a continuing effort to improve and refine. But these efforts seldom result in major changes in the measure of specific financial items or the net result — profits — for any substantial number of companies.

TABLE III. Before-Tax Corporate Profits Estimates: Percent Deviation of Preliminary from Final Estimates, 1948-72

	Aggregate Corporate Profits	*Communi-cations and Utilities*	*Manu-facturing*	*Finance, Insurance, and Real Estate*	*Trade and Wholesale Retail*	*Contract Con-struction*
1948	2.9	6.3	6.0	4.5	13.2	50.0
1949	1.8	0.0	2.0	22.7	24.5	0.0
1950	1.0	0.0	1.7	3.6	7.2	40.0
1951	4.0	4.0	7.2	3.4	1.8	37.5
1952	8.4	7.1	8.7	5.7	24.1	50.0
1953	6.1	2.9	2.8	2.8	25.0	16.7
1954	1.5	2.8	3.4	0.0	12.2	16.7
1955	5.0	2.5	8.7	2.5	2.1	20.0
1956	4.0	0.0	2.4	5.0	10.9	20.0
1957	0.5	2.2	2.9	7.0	4.2	75.0
1958	0.8	2.0	3.1	6.4	16.2	20.0
1959	1.5	5.6	2.0	1.8	1.8	37.5
1960	1.6	3.3	1.7	0.0	8.3	57.1
1961	3.1	4.6	7.6	0.0	2.1	0.0
1962	18.4	NA	NA	NA	NA	NA
1963	15.8	9.6	7.7	56.1	14.8	80.0
1964	NA	NA	NA	NA	NA	NA
1965	2.8	0.0	4.4	3.8	4.8	15.4
1966	4.8	0.0	0.7	3.7	4.5	0.0
1967	2.2	4.0	1.1	4.2	5.3	11.8
1968	3.8	4.9	5.9	0.0	3.6	9.5
1969	6.1	1.0	12.0	0.0	2.5	9.5
1970	1.9	2.3	6.2	5.0	0.0	18.7
1971	0.5	2.5	4.1	6.2	4.8	4.3
1972	6.8	8.3	1.6	13.1	11.1	22.2

Source: U.S Department of Commerce, *Survey of Current Business,* National Income Issues.

What Table III forcibly suggests is that the principal source of large changes in NIPA estimates is the failure adequately to adjust for changes in the Federal income tax laws as well as the inadequacy of the extrapolators for several industries. The large preliminary-to-final estimate changes in the NIPA occur, for the most part, at the time of significant changes in the tax laws. For example, the 1955 change —

5 percent — appears to be associated with the 1954 Internal Revenue Code enactment which provided major changes in the tax treatment of depreciation and the accrual of certain expenses; the 1962 and 1963 changes appear to be related to additional major changes in depreciation for tax purposes; and the 1969 change seems to be connected to the Tax Reform Act of 1969 which provided extensive tax changes.

Fundamentally, the instability of the NIPA estimates derives from BEA's practice of extrapolating past years' profits, measured by one concept of income — taxable income, using the rate of growth in profits reported in corporate financial statements which embody a different measure of income. This practice relies on the assumption that tax and book profits consistently increase or decrease in the same proportion. Given the conceptual differences among book, tax, and NIPA profits, this assumption is shaky, indeed.

Major Revisions

The NIPA have periodically undergone major revisions involving changes in the estimates for a large number of years, in contrast with the year-to-year changes in estimates described above. Since 1947, major revisions were made in 1954, 1958, 1965, and 1976. Each of these revisions has entailed statistical, definitional, and conceptual changes in one or all of the components of both sides of the NIPA. Revisions of the corporate share of national income have been substantial, frequently equal in magnitude to the error between preliminary and benchmark estimates.

Table IV shows the average absolute percentage difference between the revised and "final" benchmark estimates of profits for each major industrial classification. In general, profits estimates for industries for which corporate financial reports provide the extrapolators have been subject to smaller revisions than those for which extrapolators were based on sales data. In the comparison of the incremental effects of successive revisions shown in Table V, the same observation holds.

A considerable portion of the revision in profits each period is the result of accumulating data with respect to the effects of IRS audits for a given year's profits. Since the audit process remains incomplete for an extended period of time, there is a substantial lag in the adjustments; refined estimating techniques, however, have reduced the magnitude of this potential error. At each revision, there have also been statistical, conceptual, or definitional changes which have had a large impact on profits estimates of one or more industries.

The 1954 revision included the usual accumulated adjustments for audit; the data base previously used in estimating the effects of audit was discontinued and replaced by a new one which tended to raise the estimates; an allowance for profits of speculative builders, formerly classified as gains from sales of property, was introduced; and an improved method of estimating the profits earned from foreign branches of U.S. corporations was initiated and the rest-of-the-world category was adopted to report these earnings.

The 1958 revision was mainly statistical, involving the accumulated audit adjustment and other similar changes.

In addition to the normal statistical adjustments made in each revision, the 1965 revision introduced a change in industrial composition which substantially increased corporate profits estimates for earlier years. Mutual financial institutions were incorporated into the finance, insurance and real estate industry classification. As Table VI demonstrates, this reclassification increased that industry's profits estimate by substantial amounts — 60.7 percent in 1951. While this revision altered erratically the estimates of contract construction over the 1948-61 period, these changes had only a minor effect on aggregate corporate profits since this industry represented only a minor fraction of the total. Most of the 1965 revision is attributable to the reclassification of mutual insurance companies and to the usual minor statistical adjustments.

The 1976 revision, just completed, again involved major conceptual and definitional changes, several of which affected the corporate profits component of national income in particular, and the usual statistical adjustments. (Table VII.)

As in the case of the preliminary to "final" estimates, the changes in estimated corporated profits provided by the major revisions do not reflect on the quality of corporations' accounting procedures and practices for book purposes. They are more properly seen as measures of BEA's continuing efforts to improve its estimating procedures and to make these estimates more meaningful and useful components of the NIPA. Conceptual and statistical refinements of NIPA measures of

TABLE IV. Average Absolute Percentage Change in Profits, Major Revisions over Benchmark Estimates, by Industry, 1948-1972

	1954 Revision as % of 3rd-Year Estimates	*1958 Revision as % of 3rd-Year Estimates*	*1965 Revision as % of 3rd-Year Estimates*	*1976 Revision as % of 3rd-Year Estimates*
Aggregate Corporate Profits	3.1	1.6	7.6	6.2
Industry:				
Manfacturing	3.2	2.8	3.9	2.9
Communications and Utilities	0.5	0.6	4.6	3.4
Wholesale and Retail Trade	10.0	1.9	4.8	3.6
Finance, Insurance, and Real Estate	3.5	7.0	39.4	28.3
Services	6.7	3.3	14.9	10.6
Mining	8.6	7.9	6.4	10.1
Transportation	4.9	2.1	7.4	12.6
Contract Construction	5.6	7.6	16.6	13.0
Rest of the World	138.9	83.3	55.1	42.9

Source: U.S Department of Commerce, *Survey of Current Business,* National Income Issues and supplements to the *Survey of Current Business: National Income, 1954 Edition; U.S. Income and Output (1958); The National Income and Product Accounts of the U.S. 1929-1965;* and *The National Income and Product Accounts of the U.S. 1929-1974.*

Note: The totals were calculated as the sum of the absolute values of the percentage differences between each revision estimate and the corresponding final benchmark estimate of the annual totals divided by the number of years covered by the revision.

TABLE V. Average Absolute Percentage Change in Corporate Profits Estimates in Successive Revisions, by Industry 1948-1972

	1958 Revision as % of 1954 Revision	*1965 Revision as % of 1958 Revision*	*1976 Revision as % of 1965 Revision*
Aggregate Corporate Profits	1.6	7.4	1.1
Industry:			
Manufacturing	1.0	3.5	0.7
Communications and Utilities	1.1	4.2	0.4
Wholesale and Retail Trade	7.3	4.2	0.9
Finance, Insurance and Real Estate	12.6	40.7	4.5
Services	10.0	16.5	2.1
Mining	5.2	7.5	6.7
Transportation	2.6	3.0	0.9
Contract Construction	3.3	22.5	1.5
Rest of the World	0.0	0.0	0.6

Source: U.S Department of Commerce, *Survey of Current Business,* National Income Issues and supplements to the *Survey of Current Business: National Income, 1954 Edition; U.S. Income and Output (1958); The National Income and Product Accounts of the U.S. 1929-1965;* and *The National Income and Product Accounts of the U.S. 1929-1974.*

Note: The figures were computed as the sum of the absolute values of the percentage changes between the estimates of the 1958, 1965, and 1976 revisions and those of the immediately preceeding revision for each annual total, divided by the number of years covered by the successive revision.

corporate profits, no matter how large the resulting change in the estimates, do not imply that corresponding revisions in book and tax concepts and measures of profits are called for; these measures serve differing purposes. Rather, major revisions in the NIPA estimates should be the occasion for reminders to the users of these data of the significant differences in concept and measure and for cautions against interpreting the changes in estimates as indications of corresponding changes in past measures of book profits.

TABLE VI. Percentage Change, 1965 Revisions over Benchmark Estimates, Selected Industries, 1948-1963

	Aggregate Corporate Profits	*Communications and Utilities*	*Manufacturing*	*Finance, Insurance, and Real Estate*	*Wholesale and Retail Trade*	*Contract Construction*
1948	4.1	6.7	0.0	47.8	0.0	0.0
1949	6.6	5.9	0.7	44.4	0.0	0.0
1950	3.9	0.0	0.4	41.4	0.0	0.0
1951	6.6	7.7	2.9	60.7	1.9	20.0
1952	8.4	3.3	5.0	48.5	2.3	0.0
1953	9.7	3.0	7.1	48.6	2.6	0.0
1954	14.3	5.7	9.8	56.8	5.6	20.0
1955	8.2	4.9	4.2	46.3	6.1	25.0
1956	9.2	4.7	4.4	47.6	3.9	16.7
1957	9.3	6.8	5.0	41.3	8.7	14.3
1958	10.7	4.2	5.4	40.0	9.3	16.7
1959	9.2	5.3	3.5	43.1	7.3	40.0
1960	12.2	6.5	6.2	41.9	13.6	66.7
1961	13.8	12.9	7.3	51.7	12.8	50.0
1962	NA	NA	NA	NA	NA	NA
1963	0.0	0.0	0.0	0.0	0.0	0.0

Source: U.S Department of Commerce, *Survey of Current Business,* National Income Issues and *The National Income and Product Accounts of the U.S., 1929-1965,* a supplement to the *Survey of Current Business.*

TABLE VII. Percentage Change, 1976 Revision over Benchmark Estimates, Selected Industries, 1948-1973

	Aggregate Corporate Profits	*Communi-cations and Utilities*	*Manu-facturing*	*Finance, Insurance, and Real Estate*	*Wholesale and Retail Trade*	*Contract Con-struction*
1948	4.1	6.7	0.0	43.5	0.0	0.0
1949	6.6	5.9	0.7	44.4	0.0	0.0
1950	3.9	0.0	0.4	37.9	0.0	0.0
1951	6.6	7.7	2.9	60.7	1.9	20.0
1952	8.4	3.3	5.0	48.5	2.3	0.0
1953	9.7	3.0	7.1	49.5	2.6	0.0
1954	14.3	5.7	9.8	51.3	5.6	20.0
1955	8.2	4.9	4.2	41.5	6.1	25.0
1956	9.2	4.7	4.4	42.9	3.9	16.7
1957	9.3	6.8	5.0	37.0	8.7	14.3
1958	9.9	4.2	5.4	34.0	9.3	16.7
1959	8.2	5.3	3.1	37.9	7.3	40.0
1960	9.5	6.5	4.4	35.5	11.4	66.7
1961	10.0	9.7	4.6	41.4	6.4	50.0
1962	NA	NA	NA	NA	NA	NA
1963	2.9	0.0	1.8	9.0	3.2	11.1
1964	3.1	1.2	2.4	8.7	3.8	8.7
1965	3.3	1.1	2.0	11.0	2.3	6.7
1966	4.2	1.0	2.1	10.7	4.3	5.9
1967	3.1	1.1	1.0	7.9	3.0	5.3
1968	2.3	1.0	0.9	6.2	0.9	0.0
1969	1.8	1.0	0.8	8.0	0.8	5.3
1970	3.4	1.2	1.3	7.4	1.7	0.0
1971	1.9	0.0	0.9	8.9	0.8	0.0
1972	4.6	0.0	0.0	0.0	0.0	0.0

Source: U.S. Department of Commerce, *Survey of Current Business*, National Income Issues, and *The National Income and Product Accounts of the U.S., 1929-74*, a supplement to the *Survey of Current Business.*

Recommendations for Improving the NIPA Estimates of Corporate Profits

The problems associated with frequent and often substantial changes in the NIPA estimates of corporate profits are serious enough to warrant major efforts materially to reduce if not to eliminate these changes. Achieving this objective, however, is likely to require drastic changes in BEA estimating procedures; in the very nature of the case, these changes are not in prospect in the near future.

The most fundamental of these changes would be substantially to divorce the NIPA estimates from the IRS tax measures. As the discussion above points out, profits data obtained from company reports have the significant advantage, compared with tax return data, of substantial year-to-year consistency in concept and measurement. To be sure, book profits differ materially from NIPA profits, but the adjustments required to convert the former to the latter do not appear to be more complex or extensive than the adjustments of tax return information upon which BEA now principally relies. Moreover, using book profits as the fundamental data source would materially reduce the problems which now arise in using this measure to extrapolate a quite different measure — tax return profits — as a means of estimating yet a third measure — NIPA profits. Assuming BEA could adequately resolve the conceptual and statistical adjustment problems in going from book to NIPA profits, the same source — book profits — could be relied upon both for benchmark adjustments and inter-benchmark adjustments. And since "final" books profits do not lag anywhere near so substantially behind preliminary estimates as do the respective IRS tax return estimates, the number of adjustments and the period over which they are spread would be reduced.

It might be argued that whatever the year-to-year inconsistencies in tax return data, for any given year profits estimates drawn from this source are likely to be more consistent from company to company than data drawn from company reports. Presumably this should be true because the tax return data must reflect compliance by all companies with the statutes and regulations applicable in the given year, whereas corporate financial reports are so constrained to a far lesser extent. In fact, however, the tax laws and regulations in any given year afford taxpayers in differing situations an enormous degree of latitude in the measurement of various types of revenues and costs. Business accounting for book purposes, on the other hand, is extensively governed by standardized accounting principles. If anything, there is probably a higher degree of cross-sectional consistency in book than in tax-return measures of profits. Moreover, cross-sectional differences in book measures are likely to reflect significant and real differences in company and industry situations and results, whereas with the IRS cross-sectional differences must also reflect differences in applicable tax provisions.

The most serious reservation at the present time and for the near future against shifting to book profits as the basic source of NIPA profits estimates is the present lack of uniform and reliable samples among industries. Major improvements would be required in the FTC sample of manufacturing, mining, and wholesale and retail trade companies if these data were to serve as the basic inputs to the NIPA estimates. For other industries, even more extensive and complex changes in sampling procedures would be required, very possibly entailing substantial costs both for the Government and for the sampled companies.

Development of statistically more refined and more extensive samples of the book profits in the industries for which they are not presently available would also facilitate and improve BEA's extrapolation of profits estimates for the periods between "final" book profits availability — primarily for quarterly estimates. In this respect, too, BEA would be advantaged by the use of conceptually consistent data, rather than having to rely, as at present, on a variety of indicators and their respective relationships to tax and NIPA measures of profits.

A number of income and cost components would probably be better measured than at present, for NIPA purposes, directly from corporate financial statements. For example, instalment sales should be measured in NIPA as the full amount of the sales in a given year rather than that year's actual receipts with respect to such sales. As indicated earlier, standard accounting practice generally accords with the conceptually correct treatment of such sales, while tax returns more generally include only an aliquot portion of each year's sales in the year's revenues. BEA attempts to adjust the tax return measures to the NIPA concept, but the data available for doing so are fragmentary and therefore unreliable.

Similarly, since the 1976 major revision, NIPA measures of capital consumption allowances are based on highly arbitrary assumptions as to useful life and time paths of depreciation of depreciable assets. This necessarily produces an artificial uniformity among companies and industries whose actual depreciation experience, even in the context of the NIPA concept, is far more diverse. Apart from the use of historical rather than replacement cost as the basis, book depreciation, while far from identical to NIPA capital recovery allowances, is sufficiently akin in basic concept to the latter to warrant its use as the principal data input for the NIPA measure. Accounting practice, to be sure, tends to conventionalize depreciation for book purposes; in some cases, this results in excessively conservative, in others, too liberal depreciation allowances. Nevertheless, it allows sufficient leeway to reflect differences among companies in expected durability and economic longevity and in the time pattern of the conversion of prepaid to current expense as to allow more realistic measures than currently provided in the NIPA.

The switch from tax returns to corporate financial statements as the fundamental data source need not entirely eliminate the former as an input into BEA's estimates of NIPA profits. Tax return data might be employed at reasonable intervals — perhaps every 3 or 5 years, perhaps more frequently — as a means of examining the adequacy of the various industry samples proposed above. Every effort, obviously, should be made to take advantage of the data base and sampling capacity involved in IRS's preparation of *Statistics of Income*. The proposed use should be expected to produce continuing improvement in the industry samples urged above, without entailing the problems of differences in concept and measures in the current procedures for producing NIPA estimates of corporate profits.

As suggested, any such change in estimation procedures should not realistically be anticipated in the near future. Pending such changes, if indeed there is no serious impediment thereto, a number of things can be done to avert or to mitigate the misinterpretation and confusion arising from the frequent revisions of NIPA profits estimates.

For one thing, BEA should be at pains to call to the attention of the consumers of these data the fact that the NIPA concept and measure of corporate profits differ materially from book and tax concepts and measures. In doing so, it should stress the differences in purpose for which profits are measured. It should be at equal pains to point out that changes and revisions in the NIPA estimates do not reflect corresponding changes in book measures and that the NIPA changes do not imply anything whatever about the reliability of individual companies' financial statements. It should emphasize that its estimates are provisional and subject to (possibly substantial) changes, not because of the provisional character or variability of corporate financial statements, but because of BEA's estimating procedures and its continuing efforts to improve them. It should develop and publish statistical measures of the variance and errors of its estimates as a quantitative indication for consumers of the likely range of change in its estimates.

Such a statement of these caveats is not proposed in the spirit of demeaning the organization's efforts nor the quality of its output. The intent, instead, is to make the estimates more useful by informing their consumers of their limitations. Avoiding abuse of the data because of ignorance or misinterpretation of their content is a wholesome objective to be pursued by those who prepare these estimates, completely in the spirit which BEA has always shown in its continuing efforts to advance the usefulness of its output.

NOTES

NOTES

NOTES

NOTES

NOTES

NOTES